*Essays on
Ancient Magic*

By Helena P. Blavatsky

Copyright © 2021 Lamp of Trismegistus. All rights reserved. No part of this publication may be reproduced or transmitted in any form or by any means, electronic or mechanical, including photocopying, recording, or by any information storage and retrieval system, without permission in writing from Lamp of Trismegistus. Reviewers may quote brief passages.

ISBN: 978-1-63118-535-9

Esoteric Classics

Other Books in this Series and Related Titles

The Use of Evil by Annie Besant (978-1-63118-532-8)

The Historic, Mythic and Mystic Christ by Annie Besant (978-1-63118-533-5)

Aurora of the Philosophers by Paracelsus (978-1-63118-507-6)

The Hidden Mysteries of Christianity by Annie Besant (978–1–63118–534–2)

Clairvoyance and Psychic Abilities by A Besant &c (978-1-63118-403-1)

The Feminine Occult by various authors (978-1-63118-711-7)

Alchemy in the Nineteenth Century by Helena P Blavatsky (978-1-63118-446-8)

Essays on the Esoteric Tradition of Karma by A Besant &c (978-1-63118-426-0)

Rosicrucian Rules, Secret Signs, Codes and Symbols by various (978-1-63118-488-8)

An Outline of Theosophy by C W Leadbeater (978-1-63118-452-9)

Paracelsus, the Four Elements and Their Spirits by M P Hall (978-1-63118-400-0)

The Stone of the Philosophers by A E Waite (978-1-63118-509-0)

The Rosicrucian Chemical Marriage by Christian Rosenkreuz (978-1-63118-458-1)

The Alchemical Catechism of Paracelsus by Paracelsus (978-1-63118-513-7)

Qabbalistic Teachings and the Tree of Life by M P Hall (978-1-63118-482-6)

History, Analysis and Secret Tradition of the Tarot by Hall &c (978-1-63118-445-1)

Crystal Vision Through Crystal Gazing by Frater Achad (978-1-63118-455-0)

Arcane Formulas or Mental Alchemy by W W Atkinson (978-1-63118-459-8)

The Machinery of the Mind by Dion Fortune (978-1-63118-451-2)

The A E Waite Reader: A Selection of Occult Essays (978-1-63118-515-1)

The Leadbeater Reader: A Selection of Occult Essays (978-1-63118-483-3)

Audio versions are also available on Audible, Amazon and Apple

Other Books in this Series and Related Titles

On the Cave of the Nymphs in the Odyssey by Thomas Taylor (978-1-63118-505-2)

Occult Symbolism of Animals, Insects, Reptiles, Fish & Birds (978-1-63118-420-8)

The Poem of Hashish by A Crowley & C Baudelaire (978-1-63118-484-0)

Brothers & Builders by Joseph Fort Newton (978-1-63118-506-9)

The Kabbalah of Masonry & Related Writings by E Levi &c (978-1-63118-453-6)

A Collection of Fiction and Essays by Occult Writers on Supernatural and Metaphysical Subjects by various (978–1–63118–510–6)

The Sepher Yetzirah and the Qabalah by M P Hall (978-1-63118-481-9)

Cloud Upon the Sanctuary by Waite & K Eckartshausen (978-1-63118-438-3)

The Hymns of Hermes by G R S Mead (978-1-63118-405-5)

The Secrets of Enoch by Enoch (978-1-63118-449-9)

The Golden Verses of Pythagoras: Five Translations (978-1-63118-479-6)

The Devil in Love by Jacques Cazotte (978–1–63118–499–4)

The Eleusinian Mysteries and Rites by Dudley Wright (978–1–63118–530–4)

Gnosis of the Mind by G. R. S. Mead (978-1-63118-408-6)

The First and Second Gospels of the Infancy of Jesus Christ (978-1-63118-415-4)

The Life of Pythagoras by Porphyry (978-1-63118-512-0)

Freemasonry & Catholicism by Max Heindel (978-1-63118-508-3)

Rosicrucians and Speculative Masonry in the Seventeenth Century (978-1-63118-489-5)

The Influence of Pythagoras on Freemasonry and Other Essays (978-1-63118-404-8)

The Path of Light: A Manual of Maha-Yana Buddhism (978-1-63118-471-0)

Tao Te Ching & Commentary by Lao Tzu & C Johnston (978-1-63118-495-6)

Audio versions are also available on Audible, Amazon and Apple

Table of Contents

Introduction…7

Ancient Egyptian Magic…9

Animated Statues…23

Black Magic in Science…35

African Magic…53

INTRODUCTION

The word "esoteric" can be difficult to define. Esotericism in general can be seen less as a system of beliefs and more as a category, which encompasses numerous, different systems of beliefs. It's a bit of juxtaposition, since the word "esoteric" indicates something that few people know about, while the term itself broadly covers numerous philosophies, practices, areas of study and belief systems.

In a greater sense, Esotericism acts as a storehouse for secret knowledge, which is often considered ancient (by *tradition, if not by fact),* passed down from generation to generation, in private. At various times in history, simply possessing the knowledge of some of these subjects, was considered illegal and a jailable offence, if discovered. This usually included such general topics as Alchemy, Pharmacology, Qabalah, Hermeticism, Occultism, Ceremonial Magic, Astrology, Divination, Rosicrucianism and so on. Collectively, these areas of study were often referred to as the esoteric sciences.

Sometimes, the outer garment of a subject isn't esoteric, while what is hidden beneath it, is. As an example, Freemasonry isn't necessarily esoteric by nature (at *least not anymore),* but certain signs, passwords and handshakes given to the candidate during their initiation, are in fact, esoteric, in the sense that they are hidden from the general public.

Today, in the twenty-first century, such topics are readily available at bookstores across the country, and numerous mainsteam publishers offer beginners guides and coffee-table volumes on many of these subjects, intended for mass appeal. Books like *"The Secret"* have turned previously arcane topics into household knowledge. All that being the case, however, it isn't to say that there still aren't buried secrets to uncover, ancient wisdom being ignored and forgotten mysteries to be explored. In fact, it is often that we are only able to further our own studies by standing on the shoulders of these disappearing giants.

Lamp of Trismegistus is doing its part to help preserve humanity's esoteric history by making some of these classics available to those students who are seeking to unearth the knowledge of these ancient colossi.

So, be sure to check other titles from our *Esoteric Classics* series, as well as our *Occult Fiction, Theosophical Classics, Foundations of Freemasonry Series, Supernatural Fiction, Paranormal Research Series, Studies in Buddhism* and our *Christian Apocrypha Series*. You can also download the audio versions of most of these titles from Amazon, Apple or Audible, for learning on the go.

ANCIENT EGYPTIAN MAGIC

Paulthier, the French Indianist, may, or may not, be taxed with too much enthusiasm when saying that India appears before him as the grand and primitive focus of human thought, whose steady flame has ended by communicating itself to, and setting on fire the whole ancient world — yet, he is right in his statement. It is Aryan metaphysics that have led the mind to occult knowledge — the oldest and the mother science of all, since it contains within itself all the other sciences. And it is Occultism — the synthesis of all the discoveries in nature and, chiefly, of the psychic potency within and beyond every physical atom of matter — that has been the primitive bond that has cemented into one corner-stone the foundations of all the religions of antiquity.

The primitive spark has set on fire every nation, truly, and Magic underlies now every national faith, whether old or young. Egypt and Chaldea are foremost in the ranks of those countries that furnish us with the most evidence upon the subject, helpless as they are to do as India does — to protect their paleo-graphic relics from desecration. The turbid waters of the canal of Suez carry along to those that wash the British shores, the magic of the earliest days of Pharaonic Egypt, to fill up with its crumbled dust the British, French, German and Russian museums. Ancient, *historical* Magic is thus reflecting itself upon the scientific records of our own all-denying century. It forces the hand and tires the brain of the scientist, laughing at his efforts to interpret its meaning in his own materialistic way, yet helps the Occultist better to understand modern Magic, the rickety, weak grandchild of her powerful, archaic grandam. Hardly a hieratic papyrus exhumed along with the swathed mummy of King or Priest-Hierophant, or a weather-beaten, indecipherable inscription from the tormented sites of Babylonia or

Nineveh, or an ancient tile-cylinder — that does not furnish new food for thought or some suggestive information to the student of Occultism. Withal, magic is denied and termed the "superstition" of the ignorant ancient philosopher.

Thus, magic in every papyrus; magic in all the religious formulae; magic bottled up in hermetically closed vials, many thousands of years old; magic in elegantly bound, modern works; magic in the most popular novels; magic in social gatherings; magic — worse than that, SORCERY — in the very air one breathes in Europe, America, Australia: the more civilised and cultured a nation, the more formidable and effective the effluvia of unconscious magic it emits and stores away in the surrounding atmosphere.

Tabooed, derided, magic would, of course, never be accepted under her legitimate name; yet science has begun dealing with that ostracised science under modern masks, and very considerably. But what is in a name? Because a wolf is scientifically defined as an animal of the *genus canis,* does it make of him a dog? Men of science may prefer to call the magic inquired into by Porphyry and explained by Iamblichus *hysterical hypnosis,* but that does not make it the less magic. The result and outcome of primitive *Revelation* to the earlier races by their "*Divine* Dynasties" the *king-instructors,* became *innate* knowledge in the Fourth race, that of the Atlanteans; and that knowledge is now called in its rare cases of "abnormal" genuine manifestations *mediumship.* The secret history of the world preserved only in far-away, secure retreats, would alone, if told unreservedly, inform the present generations of the powers that lie latent, and to most unknown, in man and nature. It was the fearful misuse of magic by the Atlanteans, that let their race to utter destruction, and — to oblivion. The tale of their sorcery and wicked enchantments has reached us, through classical writers, in fragmentary bits, as legends and childish fairy-tales, and as fathered on smaller nations.

Thence the scorn for necromancy, goëtic magic, and theurgy. The "witches" of Thessaly are not less laughed at in our day than the modern medium or the credulous Theosophist. This is again due to *sorcery,* and one should never lack the moral courage to repeat the term; for it is the fatally abused magic that forced the adepts, "the Sons of Light", to bury it deep, after its sinful votaries had themselves found a watery grave at the bottom of the ocean; thus placing it beyond the reach of the profane of the race that succeeded to the Atlanteans. It is, then, to sorcery that the world is indebted for its present ignorance about it. But who or what class in Europe or America, will believe the report? With one exception, none; and that exception is found in the Roman Catholics and their clergy; but even they, while bound by their religious dogmas to credit its existence, attribute to it a satanic origin. It is this theory which, no doubt, has to this day prevented magic from being dealt with scientifically.

Still, *nolens volens,* science has to take it in hand. Archaeology in its most interesting department — Egyptology and Assyriology — is fatally wedded to it, do what it may. For magic is so mixed up with the world's history that, if the latter is ever to be written at all in its completeness, giving the truth and *nothing* but the truth, there seems to be no help for it. If Archaeology counts still upon discoveries and reports upon hieratic writings that will be free from the hateful subject, then HISTORY will never be written, we fear.

One sympathises profoundly with, and can well imagine, the embarrassing position of the various savants and "F.R.S." of Academicians and Orientalists. Forced to decipher, translate and interpret old mouldy papyri, inscriptions on steles and Babylonia *rhombs,* they find themselves at every moment face to face with MAGIC! Votive offerings, carvings, hieroglyphics, incantations — the whole paraphernalia of that hateful "superstition" — state them in the eyes, demand their attention, fill them with the most disagreeable perplexity. Only think what must be their feelings in the following case in hand. An evidently precious papyrus is exhumed. It is the *post-mortem* passport furnished to the osirified soul of a just translated Prince or even Pharaoh, written in red and black characters by a learned and famous scribe, say of the Fourth Dynasty, under the supervision of an Egyptian Hierophant — a class considered in all the ages and held by posterity as the most learned of the learned, among the ancient sages and philosophers. The statement therein were written at the solemn hours of the death and burial of a King Hierophant, of a Pharaoh and ruler. The purpose of the paper is the introduction of the "soul" to the awful region of Amenti, before its judges, there where a lie is said to outweigh every other crime The Orientalist carries away the papyrus and devotes to its interpretation days, perhaps weeks, of labour, only to find in it the following statement: "In the thirteenth year and the second month of *Schomoo* in the twenty-eight day of the same, we, the first High-priest of Ammon, the king of the gods, Penotman, the son of the delegate (or substitute) for the High-priest Pionki-moan, and the scribe of the temple of Sosser-sookhons and of the Necropolis Bootegamonmoo, began to dress the late Prince Oozirmari Pionokha, etc., etc., preparing him for eternity. When ready, *the mummy was pleased to arise and thank his servants, as also to accept a cover worked for him by the hand of the "lady singer", Nefrelit Nimutha, gone into eternity the year so and so -"* some hundred years before!" The whole in hieroglyphics.

This may be mistaken reading. There are dozens of papyri, though, well authenticated and recording more curious readings and narratives than that corroborated in this, by Sanchoniaton and Manetho, by Herodotus and Plato, Syncellus and dozens of other writers and philosophers, who mention the subject. Those papyri note down very often, as seriously as any historical fact needing no special corroboration, whole dynasties of Kings' — *manes,* viz., of *phantoms and ghosts.* The same is found in the histories of other nations.

All claim for their first and earliest dynasties *(The Secret Doctrine* teaches that those dynasties were composed of divine beings, "the ethereal images of human creatures", in reality "gods", in their luminous astral bodies; the *Sishta* of preceding manvantaras) of rulers and kings, what the Greeks called *Manes* and the Egyptians *Ourvagan,* "gods", etc.. Rossellius has tried to interpret the puzzling statement but in vain. "The word *manes* meaning *urvagan",* he says, "and that term in its literal sense signifying *exterior image,* we may suppose, if it were possible to bring down that dynasty within some historical period — that the word referred to *some form of theocratic governments represented by the images of the gods and priests"*!!

A dynasty of, to all appearance, *living,* at all events acting and ruling, kings turning out to have been simply mannikins and images, would require, to be accepted, a far wider stretch of modern credulity than even "kings' phantoms".

Were these Hierophants and Scribes, Pharaohs and King-Initiates all fools or frauds, confederates and liars, to have either believed themselves or tried to make other people believe in such cock-and-bull stories, if there were no truth at the foundation? And that for a long series of millenniums, from the first to the last Dynasty?

Of the *divine* Dynasty of *Manes,* the test of the *Secret Doctrine* will treat more fully; but a few such feats may be recorded from genuine papyri and the discoveries of archaeology. The Orientalists have found a plank of salvation: though forced to publish the contents of some famous papyri, they now call them *Romances* of the days of Pharaoh so-and-so. The device is ingenious, if not absolutely honest. The literary Sadducees may fairly rejoice.

One of such is the so-called "Lepsius Papyrus" of the Berlin Museum, now purchased by the latter from the heirs of Richard Lepsius. It is written in hieratic characters in the archaic Egyptian (old Coptic) tongue, and is considered one of the most important archaeological discoveries of our age, inasmuch as it furnishes dates for comparison, and rectifies several mistakes in the order of dynastical successions. Unfortunately its *most important fragments are missing*. The learned Egyptologists who had the greatest difficulty in deciphering it have concluded that it was "an historical romance of the sixteenth century B.C., dating back to events that took place during the reign of Pharaoh Cheops, the supposed builder of the pyramid of that name, who flourished in the twenty-sixth century before our era". It shows Egyptian life and the state of society at the Court of that great Pharaoh, nearly nine hundred years before the little unpleasantness between Joseph and Mrs. Potiphar.

The first scene opens with King Cheops on his throne, surrounded by his sons, whom he commands to entertain him with narratives about hoary antiquity and the miraculous powers exercised by the celebrated sages and magicians at the Court of his predecessor. Prince Chefren than tells his audience how a *magus* during the epoch of Pharaoh Nebkha fabricated a crocodile out of wax and endowed him with life and *obedience*. Having been placed by a husband in the room of his faithless spouse, the crocodile snapped at both the wife and her lover, and seizing them carried them both into the sea. Another prince told a story of his grandfather, the parent of Cheops, Pharaoh Senefru. Feeling seedy, he commanded a magician into his presence, who advised him as a remedy the spectacle of twenty beautiful maidens of the Court sporting in a boat on the lake near by. The maidens obeyed and the hear of the old despot was "refreshed". But suddenly one of the ladies screamed and began to weep aloud. She had dropped into the water, one hundred and twenty feet deep in that spot, a rich necklace. Then a magician pronounced a formula, called the genii of the air and water to his help, and plunging his hand into the waves brought back with it the necklace. The pharaoh was greatly struck with the feat. He looked no more at the twenty beauties, "divested of their clothes, covered with nets, and with twenty oars made of ebony and gold"; but commanded that sacrifices should be made to the *manes* of those two magicians when they died. To this Prince Gardadathu remarked that the highest among such magicians *never die*, and one of them lived to that day, more than a centenarian, at the town of Deyd-Snefroo; that his name was Deddy; and that he had the miraculous power of reuniting cut-off heads to their bodies and recalling the whole to life, as also full authority and sway over the lions of the desert. He, Deddy, knew likewise where to procure the needed expensive materials for the temple of the god Thoth (the *wisdom* deity), which edifice Pharaoh Cheops was anxious to raise near his great pyramid. Upon hearing this, the mighty King Cheops expressed a desire to see the old sage at his Court! Thereupon the Prince Gardadathu started on his journey, and brought back with him the great magician.

After long greetings and mutual compliments and obeisance, according to the papyrus, a long conversation ensued between the Pharaoh and the sage, which goes on briefly thus:

"I am told, oh sage, that thou art able to reunite heads severed from their bodies to that latter."

"I can do so, great King", answered Deddy.

"Let a criminal be brought here, without delay", quoth the Pharaoh.

"Great Kind, my power does not extend to men. I can resurrect only animals", remarked the sage.

A goose was then brought, its head cut off and placed in the east corner of the hall, and its body at the western side. Deddy extended his arm in the two directions in turn and muttered a magic formula. Forthwith the body of the bird arose and walked to the center of the hall, and the head rolled up to meet it. Then the head jumped on the bleeding neck; the two were reunited; and the goose began to walk about, none the worse for the operation of beheading.

The same wonderful feat was repeated by Deddy upon canaries and a bull. After which the Pharaoh desired to be informed with regard to the projected temple of Thoth.

The sage-magician knew all about the old remains of the temple, hidden in a certain house a Heliopolis: but he had no right to reveal it to the king. The revelation had to come from the eldest of the three triplets of Rad-Dedtoo. "The latter is the wife of the priest of the Sun, at the city of Saheboo. She will conceive the triplet-sons from the sun-god, and these children will play an important part in the history of the land of Khemi (Egypt), inasmuch as they will be called to rule it. The eldest, before he becomes a Pharaoh, will be High-priest of the Sun at the city of Heliopolis.

"Upon hearing this, Pharaoh Cheops rent his clothes in grief: his dynasty would thus be overthrown by the son of the deity to whom he was actually raising a temple!"

Here the papyrus is torn; and a large portion of it being missing, posterity is denied the possibility of learning what Pharaoh Cheops undertook in this emergency.

The fragment that follows apprises us of that which is evidently the chief subject of the archaic record — the birth of the three sons of the sun-god. As soon as Rad-Dedtoo felt the pangs of childbirth, the great sun-god called the goddesses Isis, Nephthys, Mesehentoo, and Hekhtoo, and sent them to help the priestess, saying: "She is in labour with my three sons who will, one day, be the rulers of this land. Help her, and they will raise temples for you, will make innumerable libations of wine and sacrifices". The goddesses did as they were asked, and three boys, each one yard long and *with very long arms,* were born. Isis gave them their names and Nephthys blessed them, while the two other goddesses confirmed on them their glorious future. The three young men became eventually kings of the Fifth Dynasty, their names being Ouserkath, Sagoorey and Kakaÿ. After the goddesses had returned to their celestial mansions some great miracles occurred. The corn given the mother goddesses returned of itself into the corn-bin in an outhouse of the High-priest, and the servants reported that voices of invisibles were singing in it the hymns sung at the birth of hereditary princes, and the sounds of music and dances belonging to that rite were distinctly heard. This phenomenon endangered, later on, the lives of the future kings — the triplets.

A female slave having been punished once by the High-priestess, the former ran away from the house, and spoke thus to the assembled crowds: " How dare she punish me, that woman who gave birth to three kings? I will go and notify it to Pharaoh Cheops, our lord."

At this interesting place the papyrus is again torn; and the reader left once more in ignorance of what resulted from the denunciation, and how the three boy-pretenders avoided the persecution of the paramount ruler.

Another magical feat is given by Mariette Bey *(Mon., Dir.* pp. 1, 9, Persian epoch), from a tablet in the Bulak Museum, concerning the Ethiopian kingdom founded by the descendants of the High-priests of Ammon, wherein flourished absolute theocracy. It was the god himself, it appears, who selected the kings at his fancy, and "the *stele* 114 which is an official statement about the election of Aspalout, shows how such events took place". (Gebel-Barkal) The army gathered near the Holy Mountain at Napata, choosing six officers who had to join other delegates of state, proposed to proceed to the election of a king.

"Come", reads the inscribed legend, "come, let us choose a master who would be like an irresistible young bull". And the army began lamenting, saying — " Our master is with us, and we know him not!" And others remarked, "Aye, but we can know him, though till now no one save Râ (the god) does so: may the great God protect him from harm wherever he be".... .... Forthwith the whole army cried out, "But there is that god Ammon-Râ, in the Holy Mountain, and he is the god of Ethiopia! Let us to him, do not speak in ignorance of him; for the word spoken in ignorance of him is not good. Let him choose, that god, who is the god of the kingdom of Ethiopia, since the days of Râ.... He will guide us, as the Ethiopian kings are all his handiwork, and he gives the kingdom to the son whom he loves." "This is what the entire army saith: 'It is an excellent speech, in truth a million of times.' "

Then the narrative shows the delegates duly purified, proceeding to the temple and prostrating themselves before the huge statue of Ammon-Râ, while framing their request. "The Ethiopic priests are mighty ones. They know how to fabricate miraculous images and status, capable of motion and speech, to serve as vehicles for the gods; it is an art they hold from their Egyptian ancestors."

All the members of the Royal family pass in procession before the statue of Ammon-Râ — still it moveth not. Bus as soon as Aspalout approaches it, the huge statue seizes him with both arms, and loudly exclaims: "This is your king! This is your master who will make you live!"' and the army chiefs greet the new Pharaoh. He enters into the sanctuary and is crowned by the god, personally, and with his own hands; then joins his army. The festival ends with the distribution of bread and beer. (Gebel-Barkal)

There is a number of papyri and old inscriptions proving beyond the slightest doubt that for thousands of years high-priests, magicians and Pharaohs *believed* — as well as the masses — in magic, besides practicing it; the latter being liable to be referred to clever jugglery. The statues *had* to be *fabricated;* for unless they were made of certain elements and stones, and were prepared under certain constellations, in accordance with the conditions prescribed by magic art, the *divine* (or *infernal,* if some will so have it) powers, or FORCES , that were expected to animate such statues and images, could not be made to act therein. A galvanic-battery has to be prepared of specific metals and materials, not made at random, if one would have it produce *its* magical effects. A photograph has to be obtained under specific conditions of darkness and certain chemicals, before it can result in a given purpose.

Some twenty years ago, archaeology was enriched with a very curious Egyptian document giving the views of that ancient religion upon the subject of ghosts *(manes)* and magic in general. It is called the "Harris papyrus on Magic" (Papyrus Magique). It is extremely curious in its bearing upon the esoteric teachings of Occult Theosophy, and is very suggestive. It is left for our next article [Animated Statues] — on Magic.

ANIMATED STATUES

To whatsoever cause it may be due matters little, but the word *fetich* is given in the dictionaries the restricted sense of "an object selected temporarily for worship," "a small idol used by the African *savages*," etc., etc.

In his "Des Cultes Anterieurs à l'Idolatrie," Dulaure defines Fetichism as "the adoration of an object considered by the ignorant and the weak-minded as the receptacle or the habitation of a god or genius."

Now all this is extremely erudite and profound, no doubt; but it lacks the merit of being either true or correct. Fetich may be an *idol* among the negroes of Africa, according to Webster; and there are weak-minded and ignorant people certainly who are fetich worshippers. Yet the theory that certain objects—statues, images, and *amulets* for example—serve as a temporary or even constant habitation to a "god," "genius" or *spirit* simply, has been shared by some of the most intellectual men known to history. It was *not* originated by the ignorant and weak-minded, since the majority of the world's sages and philosophers, from *credulous* Pythagoras down to sceptical Lucian, believed in such a thing in antiquity; as in our highly civilized, cultured and learned century several hundred millions of Christians still believe in it, whether the above definitions be correct or the one we shall now give. The administration of the Sacrament, the mystery of Transubstantiation "in the *supposed* conversion of the bread and wine of the Eucharist into the body and blood of Christ," would render the bread and wine and the communion cup along with them *fetiches*—no less than the tree or rag or stone of the savage African. Every miracle-working image, tomb and statue of a Saint, Virgin or Christ, in the Roman

Catholic and Greek Churches, have thus to be regarded as *fetiches;* because, whether the miracle is supposed to be wrought by God or an angel, by Christ or a saint, those images or statues *do* become—if the miracle be claimed as genuine—"the receptacle or dwelling" for a longer or shorter time of God or an "angel of God."

It is only in the "Dictionnaire des Religions" (Article on *Fetichsme*) that a pretty correct definition may be found:

"The word *fetich* was derived from the Portuguese word *fetisso*, 'enchanted,' 'bewitched' or 'charmed'; whence *fatum*, 'destiny,' *fatua*, 'fairy,'" etc.

Fetich, moreover, was and still ought to be identical with "idol"; and as the author of "The Teraphim of Idolatry" says:

"Fetichism is the adoration of *any object*, whether inorganic or living, large or of minute proportions, *in which*, or, *in connection with which*,—any 'spirit'—good or bad in short—an invisible intelligent power—has manifested its presence."

Having collected for my "Secret Doctrine" a number of notes upon this subject, I may now give some of them apropos of the latest *theosophical* novel "A Fallen Idol," and thus show that work of fiction based on some very occult truths of Esoteric Philosophy.

The images of all the gods of antiquity, from the earliest Aryans down to the latest Semites—the Jews—were all idols and fetiches, whether called *Teraphim*, *Urim* and *Thummim*, Kabeiri, or cherubs, or the gods *Lares*. If, speaking of the *teraphim*—a word that Grotius translates as "angels," an etymology authorized by Cornelius, who says that they "were the symbols of *angelic* presence"—the Christians are allowed to call them "the mediums through which *divine presence* was manifested," why not apply the same to the idols of the "heathen"?

I am perfectly alive to the fact that the modern man of science, like the average sceptic, believes no more in an "animated" image of the Roman Church than he does in the "animated" fetich of a savage. But there is no question, at present, of belief or disbelief. It is simply the evidence of antiquity embracing a period of several thousands of years, as against the denial of the XIXth century—the century of Spiritualism and Spiritism, of Theosophy and Occultism, of Charcot and his hypnotism, of psychic "suggestion," and of unrecognized BLACK MAGIC all round.

Let us Europeans honour the religion of our forefathers, by questioning it on its beliefs and their origin, before placing on its defence pagan antiquity and its grand philosophy; where do we find in Western sacred literature, so-called, the first mention of idols and fetiches? In chapter xxxi (*et seq*) of Genesis, in Ur of the Chaldees in Mesopotamia, wherein the ancestors of Abraham, Serug and Terah, worshipped little idols in clay which they called their *gods;* and where also, in Haran, Rachel stole the images (*teraphim*) of her father Laban. Jacob may have forbidden worship of those gods, yet one finds 325 years after that prohibition, the Mosaic Jews adoring "the gods of the Amorites" the same (Joshua xxiv. 14, 15). The teraphim-gods of Laban exist to this day among certain tribes of Mussulmans on Persian territory. They are small statuettes of tutelary genii, or gods, which consulted on every occasion. The Rabbis explain that Rachel no other motive for stealing her father's gods than that of preventing his learning from them the direction she and her husband Jacob had taken, lest he should prevent them from leaving home once more. Thus, it was not piety, or the fear of the Lord God of Israel, but simply a dread of the indiscretion of the gods that made her secure them. Moreover, her mandrakes were only another kind of sortilegious and magical implements.

Now what is the opinion of various classical and even sacred writers on these *idols*, which Hermes Trismegistus calls "statues foreseeing futurity" (*Asclepias*)?

Philo of Biblos shows that the Jews consulted *demons* like the Amorites, especially through small statues made of gold, shaped as nymphs which, questioned at any hour, would instruct them what the querists had to do and what to avoid. ("Antiquities"). "More Nevochim" (I, iii) it is said that nothing resembled ore those *portative and preserving* gods of the pagans (*dii portiles vel Averrunci*) than those tutelary gods of the Jews. They were "veritable phylacteries or *animated* talismans, the *spirantia simulacra* of Apuleius (Book xi), whose *answers, given* in the temple of the goddess of Syria, *were heard* by Lucian personally, and repeated by him. Kircher (the Jesuit Father) shows also that the *teraphim* looked, in quite an extraordinary way, like the pagan *Serapises* of Egypt; and Cedrenus seems to corroborate that statement of Kircher (in his Vol. iii, p. 494 "Œdipus," etc.) by show that the *t* and the *s* (like the Sanskrit *s* and the Zend *h*) were convertible letters, the *Seraphim* (or *Serapis*) and the *teraphim*, being absolute synonyms.

As to the use of these idols, Maimonides tells us ("More Nevochim," p. 41) that these gods or images passed for being endowed with the prophetic gift, and as being able to tell the people in whose possession they were "all that was useful and salutary them."

All these images, we are told, had the form of a baby or small child, others were only occasionally much larger. They were statues or regular idols in the human shape. The Chaldeans exposed them to the beams of certain planets for the latter to imbue them with their virtues and potency. These were for purposes of astromagic; the regular *teraphim* for those of necromancy and sorcery, in most cases. The spirits of the dead (elementaries) were attached to them by magic art, and they were used for various sinful purposes.

Ugolino puts in the mouth of the sage Gamaliel, St. Paul's master (or *guru*), the following words, which he quotes, he says, from his "Capito," chap. Xxxvi:

"They (the possessors of such necromantic *teraphim*) killed a new-born baby, cut off its head, and placed under its tongue, salted and oiled, a little gold lamina in which the name of *an evil* spirit was perforated; then, after suspending that head on the wall of their chamber, they lighted lamps before it, and prostrate on the ground they *conversed with it*."

The learned Marquis de Mirville believes that it was just such ex-human *fetiches* that were meant by Philostratus, who gives a number of instances of the same.

"There was the head of Orpheus"—he says—"which spoke to Cyrus, and the head of a priest-sacrificer from the temple of Jupiter Hoplosmius which, when severed from its body, revealed, as Aristotle narrates, the name of its murderer, one called Cencidas; and the head of one Publius Capitanus, which, according to Trallianus, at the moment of the victory won by Acilius the Roman Consul, over Antiochus, King of Asia, predicted to the Romans the great misfortunes that would soon befall them, etc." ("Pn. des Esprits," Vol. iii, 29 Memoir to the Academy, p. 252.)

Diodorus tells the world how such idols were fabricated for magical purposes in days of old.

"Semele, the daughter of Cadmus, having, in consequence of a fright given premature birth to a child of seven months, Cadmus, in order to follow *the custom of his country* and to give it (the babe) a *supermundane origin which would make it live after death*, enclosed its body within a gold statue, and made of it an idol for which a special cult and rites were established." (Diodorus, lib. i. p. 48.)

As Freret, in his article in the "Memoires de l'Academie des Inscriptions," Vol. xxiii, p. 247—pointedly remarks, when commenting upon the above passage:

"A singular thing, deserving still more attention, is that the said *consecration* of Semele's baby, which the *Orphics* show as having been the custom of Cadmus' ancestors—is *precisely the ceremony described by the Rabbis*, as cited by Seldenus, with regard to the *teraphim* or household gods of the Syrians and the Phœnicians. There is little probability, however, that the Jews should have been acquainted with the Orphics."

Thus, there is every reason to believe that the numerous drawings in Father Kircher's *Œdipus*, little figures and heads with metallic laminæ protruding from under their tongues, which hang entirely out of the heads' mouths, are real and genuine teraphims—as shown by de Mirville. Then again in Le Blanc's "Religions," (Vol. iii, p. 277), speaking of the Phœnician *teraphim*, the author compares them to the Greco-Phrygian *palladium*, which contained human relics. "All the mysteries of the apotheosis, of orgies, sacrifices and magic, were applied to such heads. A child young enough to have his innocent soul still united with the *Anima Mundi*—the Mundane Soul—was killed," he says; "his head was embalmed *and its soul was fixed in it, as it is averred, by the power of magic and enchantments.*" After which followed the usual process, the gold lamina, etc., etc.

Now this is terrible BLACK MAGIC, we say; and none but the *dugpas* of old, the villainous sorcerers of antiquity, used it. In the Middle Ages only several Roman Catholic priests are known to have resorted to it; among others the apostate Jacobin priest in the service of Queen Catherine of Medici, that faithful daughter of the Church of Rome and the author of the "St. Bartholomew Massacre." The story is given by Bodin, in his famous work on Sorcery "Le Demonomanie, ou Traité des Sorciers" (Paris, 1587); and it is quoted in "Isis Unveiled" (Vol. ii, p. 56). Pope Sylvester II was publicly accused by Cardinal Benno of sorcery, on account of his "Brazen Oracular Head." These heads and other *talking* statues, trophies of the magical skill of monks and bishops? were facsimiles of the *animated* gods of the ancient temples. Benedict IX, John XX, and the VIth and VIIth Popes Gregory are all known in history as sorcerers and magicians. Notwithstanding such an array of facts to show that the Latin Church has despoiled the ancient Jews of all— aye, even to their knowledge of *black art* inclusively—one of their advocates of modern times, namely, the Marquis de Mirville, is not ashamed to publish against the modern Jews, the most terrible and foul of accusations!

In his violent polemics with the French symbologists, who try to find a philosophical explanation for ancient Bible customs and rites, he says:

"We pass over the symbolic significations that are sought for to explain all such customs of the idolatrous Jews, (their *human* teraphim and severed baby-heads), because we do not believe in them (such explanations) at all. But we do believe, for one, that 'the head' consulted by the-Scandinavian Odin in every difficult affair was a *teraphim* of the same (magic) class. And that *in which we believe still more*, is, that all *those mysterious disappearances and abductions of small (Christian) children*, practised at all times and even in our own day by the Jews—*are the direct consequences of those ancient and barbarous necromantic practices* . . . Let the reader remember the incident of Damas and Father Thomas." ("Pneum des Esprits," Vol. iii, p. 254.)

Quite clear and unmistakeable this. The unfortunate, despoiled Israelites are plainly charged with abducting Christian children to behead and make *oracular* heads with them, for purposes of sorcery! Where will bigotry and intolerance with their *odium theologicum* land next, I wonder?

On the contrary, it seems quite evident that it is just in consequence of such terrible malpractices of Occultism that Moses and the early ancestors of the Jews were so strict in carrying out the severe prohibition against graven images, statues and likenesses in any shape, of either "gods" or living men. This same reason was at the bottom of the like prohibition by Mohammed and enforced by all the Mussulman prophets. For the *likeness of any person*, in whatever form and mode, of whatever material, *may be turned into a deadly weapon against the original by a really learned practitioner of the black art.* Legal authorities during the Middle Ages, and even some of 200 years ago, were not wrong in putting to death those in whose possession small wax figures of their enemies were found, for it was *murder contemplated*, pure and simple. "Thou shalt not draw the *vital spirits* of thy enemy, or of any person into his *simulacrum*," for "this is a heinous crime against nature." And again: "Any object into which the *fiat* of a spirit has been drawn is dangerous, and must not be left in the hands of the ignorant. . . . An expert (in magic) has to be called purify it." ("Pract. Laws of Occult Science," Book v, Coptic copy.)

In a kind of "Manual" of Elementary Occultism, it is said: "To make a bewitched object (*fetich*) harmless, its parts have to be reduced to atoms (broken), and the whole buried in damp soil"— (follow instructions, unnecessary in a publication).

That which is called "vital spirits" is the astral body. "Souls, whether united or separated from their bodies, *have a corporeal substance inherent to their nature*," says St. Hilarion. ("Comm. in Matth." C. v. No. 8.) Now the astral body of a living person, of one unlearned in occult sciences, may be forced (by an expert in magic) to animate, or be drawn to, *and then fixed within* any object, especially into anything made in his likeness, a portrait, a statue, a little figure in wax, etc. And as whatever hits or affects the astral reacts by repercussion on the physical body, it becomes logical and stands to reason that, by stabbing the likeness in its vital parts—the heart, for instance—the original may be sympathetically killed, without any one being able to detect the cause of it. The Egyptians, who separated man (*exoterically*) into three divisions or groups—"mind body" (pure spirit, our 7th and 6th principles); the spectral soul (the 5th, 4th, and 3rd principles); and the gross body (*prana* and *sthula sarira*), called forth in their theurgies and evocations (for divine *white magical* purposes, as well as for those of the black art) the "spectral soul," or astral body, as we call it.

"It was not the soul itself that was evoked, but its *simulacrum* that the Greeks called *Eidôlon*, and which was the middle principles between soul and body. That doctrine came from the East, the cradle of all learning. The Magi of Chaldea as well as all other followers of Zoroaster, believed that it was not the *divine* soul alone (spirit) which would participate in the glory of celestial light, but also the *sensitive* soul." (Psellus, in Scholiis, in Orac.)

Translated into our Theosophical phraseology, the above refers to Atma and Buddhi—the vehicle of spirit. The Neo-Platonics, and even Origen,—"call the astral body *Augoeides* and *Astroeides*, *i.e.*, one having the brilliancy of the stars." ("Sciences Occultes," by Cte. de Resie, Vol. ii, p. 598-9.)

Generally speaking, the world's ignorance on the nature of the human phantom and vital principle, as on the functions of all man's principles, is deplorable. Whereas science denies them all—an easy way of cutting the gordian knot of the difficulty—the churches have evolved the fanciful dogma of one solitary principle, the Soul, and neither of the two will stir from its respective preconceptions, notwithstanding the evidence of all antiquity and its most intellectual writers. Therefore, before the question can be argued with any hope of lucidity, the following points have to be settled and studied by our Theosophists—those, at any rate, who are interested in the subject:

1. The difference between a physiological hallucination and a psychic or spiritual clairvoyance and clairaudience.

2. Spirits, or the entities of certain invisible beings—whether *ghosts* of once living men, angels, spirits, or elementals—have they, or have they not, a natural though an ethereal and to us invisible body? Are they united to, or can they assimilate some fluidic substance that would help them to become visible to men?

3. Have. they, or have they not, the power of so becoming infused among the atoms of any object, whether it be a statue (idol), a picture, or an amulet, as to impart to it their potency and virtue, and even to *animate* it?

4. Is it in the power of any Adept, Yogi or Initiate, *to fix* such entities, whether by *White* or *Black* magic, in certain objects?

5. What are the various conditions (save Nirvana and Avitchi) of good and bad men after death? etc., etc.

All this may be studied in the literature of the ancient classics, and especially in Aryan literature. Meanwhile, I have tried to explain and have given the collective and individual opinions thereon of all the great philosophers of antiquity in my "Secret Doctrine." I hope the book will now very soon appear. Only, in order to counteract the effects of such humoristical works as "A Fallen Idol" on weak-minded people, who see in it only a satire upon our beliefs, I thought best to give here the testimony of the ages to the effect that such *post-mortem* pranks as played by Mr. Anstey's sham ascetic, who died a sudden death, are of no rare occurrence in nature.

To conclude, the reader may be reminded that if the astral body of man is no *superstition* founded on mere hallucinations, but a reality in nature, then it becomes only logical that such an *eidôlon*, whose individuality is all centered after death in his *personal* EGO—should be attracted to the remains of the body that was his, during life; and in case the latter was burnt and the ashes buried, that it should seek to prolong its existence vicariously by either possessing itself of some living body (a medium's), or, by attaching itself to his own statue, picture, or some familiar object in the house or locality that it inhabited. The "vampire" theory, can hardly be a superstition altogether. Throughout all Europe, in Germany, Styria, Moldavia, Servia, France and Russia, those bodies of the deceased who are believed to have become *vampires*, have *special exorcismal rites* established for them by their respective Churches. Both the Greek and Latin religions think it beneficent to have such bodies dug out and transfixed to the earth by a pole of aspen-tree wood.

However it may be, whether truth or superstition, ancient philosophers and poets, classics and lay writers, have believed as we do now, and that for several thousand years in history, that man had within him his astral counterpart, which would appear by separating itself or oozing out of the gross body, during life as well as after the death of the latter. Till that moment the "spectral soul" was the vehicle of the divine soul and the pure spirit. But, as soon *as the flames had devoured* the physical envelope, the spiritual soul, separating itself from the *simulacrum* of man, ascended to its new home of unalloyed bliss (Devachan or Swarga), while the spectral eidôlon *descended* into the regions of Hades (*limbus*, purgatory, or *Kama loka*). "I have terminated my earthly career," exclaims Dido, "my glorious spectre (astral body), the IMAGE of my person, will now descend into the womb of the earth."

"Et nunc magna mei sub terras ibit imago" ("Eneid," lib. iv, 654).

Sabinus and Servius Honoratus (a learned commentator of Virgil of the VIth cent.) have taught, as shown by Delris, the demonlogian (lib. ii, ch. xx and xxv, p. 116), that man was composed, *besides his soul*, of a shadow (*umbra*) and a body. The *soul* ascends to heaven, the *body* is pulverized, and the *shadow* is plunged in Hades. . . . This phantom—*umbra seu simulacrum*—is not a *real* body, they say: it is the *appearance* of one, that no hand can touch, as it avoids contact like a breath. Homer shows this same shadow in the phantom of Patroclus, who perished, killed by Hector, and yet "Here he is—it is *his face*, his voice, his blood still flowing from his wounds!" (See "Iliad," xxiii, and also "Odyssey," i, xi.) The ancient Greeks and Latins had two souls—*anima bruta* and *anima divina*, the first of which is in Homer the animal soul, the image and the life of the body, and the second, the immortal and the divine.

As to our *Kama loka*, Ennius, says Lucrecius—"has traced the picture of the sacred regions in Acherusia, where dwell *neither our bodies nor our souls*, but only our simulacres, whose pallidity is dreadful to behold!" It is amongst those *shades* that divine Homer appeared to him, shedding bitter tears *as though the gods had created that honest man for eternal sorrow only*. It is from the midst of that world (*Kama loka*), which *seeks with avidity communication with our own*, that this *third* (part)

of the poet, his *phantom*—explained to him the mysteries of nature.
. . .

Pythagoras and Plato both divided soul into two representative parts, independent of each other—the one, the rational soul, or λόγον, the other, *irrational*, ἄλογον—the latter being again subdivided into two parts or aspects, the θυμικὸν, and the ἐπιθυμικὸν, which, with the divine soul and its spirit and the body, make the *seven* principles of Theosophy. What Virgil calls *imago*, "image," Lucretius names—*simulacrum*, "similitude" (See "De Nat. rerum" I), but they are all names for one and the same thing, the *astral body*.

We gather thus two points from the ancients entirely corroborative of our esoteric philosophy: (a) the astral or materialized figure of the dead is neither *the soul*, nor the *spirit*, nor the *body* of the deceased personage, but simply the *shadow* thereof, which justifies our calling it a "shell"; and (b) unless it be an *immortal God* (an angel) who animates an object, it can never be a *spirit*, to wit, the SOUL, or real, spiritual ego of a once living man; for these ascend, and an astral shadow (unless it be of a living person) can never be higher than a terrestrial, *earth-bound* ego, or an *irrational* shell. Homer was therefore right in making Telemachus exclaim, on seeing Ulysses, who reveals himself to his son: "No, thou art not my father, thou art a demon, a spirit who flatters and deludes me!"

Οὐσὺγ' Ὀδυσσεὺσ εσσι πατηρ εμὸσ ἀλλάμε δαἰμων Θέλγει.("Odyssey," xvi, 194.)

It is such illusive shadows, belonging to neither Earth nor Heaven, that are used by sorcerers and other adepts of the Black Art, to help them in persecutions of victims; to hallucinate the minds of very honest and well meaning persons occasionally, who fall victims to the mental epidemics aroused by them for a purpose; and to oppose in every way the beneficent work of the guardians of mankind, whether divine or—human.

For the present, enough has been said to show that the Theosophists have the evidence of the whole of antiquity in support of the correctness of their doctrines.

BLACK MAGIC IN SCIENCE

. . . Commence research where modern conjecture closes its faithless wings (Bulwer's *Zanoni*).

The flat denial of yesterday has become the scientific axiom of to-day *(Common Sense Aphorisms)*.

Thousands of years ago the Phrygian Dactyls, the initiated priests, spoken of as the "magicians and exorcists of sickness," healed diseases by magnetic processes. It was claimed that they had obtained these curative powers from the powerful breath of Cybele, the many-breasted goddess, the daughter of Coelus and Terra. Indeed, her genealogy and the myths attached to it show Cybele as the personification and type of the vital essence, whose source was located by the ancients between the Earth and the starry sky, and who was regarded as the very *fons vitae* of all that lives and breathes. The mountain air being placed nearer to that fount fortifies health and prolongs man's existence; hence, Cybele's life, as an infant, is shown in her myth as having been preserved on a mountain. This was before that *Magna* and *Bona Dea*, the prolific *Mater*, became transformed into Ceres-Demeter, the patroness of the Eleusinian Mysteries.

Animal magnetism (*now called Suggestion and Hypnotism*) was the principal agent in theurgic mysteries as also in the *Asclepieia* – the healing temples of Aesculapius, where the patients once admitted were treated, during the process of "incubation," magnetically, during their sleep.

This creative and life-giving Force — denied and laughed at when named theurgic magic, accused for the last century of being principally based on superstition and fraud, whenever referred to as mesmerism — is now called Hypnotism, Charcotism, Suggestion, "psychology," and what not. But, whatever the expression chosen, it will ever be a loose one if used without a proper qualification. For when epitomized with all its collateral sciences — which are all sciences within *the* science — it will be found to contain possibilities the nature of which has never been even dreamt of by the oldest and most learned professors of the orthodox physical science. The latter, "authorities" so-called, are no better, indeed, than innocent bald infants, when brought face to face with the mysteries of antediluvian "mesmerism." As stated repeatedly before, the blossoms of magic, whether white or black, divine or infernal, spring all from one root. The "breath of Cybele" — Akasa tattwa, in India — is the one chief agent, and it underlay the so-called "miracles" and "supernatural" phenomena in all ages, as in every clime. As the parent-root or essence is universal, so are its effects innumerable. Even the greatest adepts can hardly say where its possibilities must stop.

The key to the very alphabet of these theurgic powers was lost after the last gnostic had been hunted to death by the ferocious persecution of the Church; and as gradually Mysteries, Hierophants, Theophany and Theurgy became obliterated from the minds of men until they remained in them only as a vague tradition, all this was finally forgotten. But at the period of the Renaissance, in Germany, a learned Theosophist, a Philosopher *per ignem,* as they called themselves, rediscovered some of the lost secrets of the Phrygian priests and of the *Asclepieia*. It was the great and unfortunate physician-Occultist, Paracelsus, the greatest Alchemist of the age. That genius it was, who during the Middle Ages was the first to publicly recommend the action of the magnet in the cure of certain diseases. Theophrastus Paracelsus – the "quack" and "drunken impostor" in the opinion of the said scientific "bald infants" of his day, and of their successors in ours – inaugurated among other things in the seventeenth century, that which has become a profitable branch in trade in the nineteenth. It is he who invented and used for the cure of various muscular and nervous diseases magnetized bracelets, armlets, belts, rings, collars and leglets; only his magnets cured far more efficaciously than do the electric belts of to-day. Van Helmont, the successor of Paracelsus, and Robert Fludd, the Alchemist and Rosicrucian, also applied magnets in the treatment of their patients. Mesmer in the eighteenth, and the Marquis de Puysegur in the nineteenth century only followed in their footsteps.

In the large curative establishment founded by Mesmer at Vienna, he employed, besides magnetism, electricity, metals and a variety of woods. His fundamental doctrine was that of the Alchemists. He believed that metals, as also woods and plants have all an affinity with and bear a close relation to, the human organism. Everything in the Universe has developed from one homogeneous primordial substance differentiated into incalculable species of matter, and everything is destined to return there into. The secret of healing, he maintained, lies in the knowledge of correspondences and affinities between kindred atoms. Find that metal, wood, stone, or plant that has the most correspondential affinity with the body of the sufferer; and, whether through internal or external use, that particular agent imparting to the patient additional strength to fight disease – (*developed generally through the introduction of some foreign element into the constitution*) – and to expel it, will lead invariably to his cure. Many and marvelous were such cures affected by Anton Mesmer. Subjects with heart disease were made well. A lady of high station, condemned to death, was completely restored to health by the application of certain sympathetic woods. Mesmer himself, suffering from acute rheumatism, cured it completely by using specially-prepared magnets.

In 1774 he too happened to come across the theurgic secret of direct vital transmission; and so highly interested was he, that he abandoned all his old methods to devote himself entirely to the new discovery. Henceforward he *mesmerised* by gaze and passes, the natural magnets being abandoned. The mysterious effects of such manipulations were called by him – *animal* magnetism. This brought to Mesmer a mass of followers and disciples. The *new* force was experimented with in almost every city and town of Europe and found everywhere an actual fact.

About 1780, Mesmer settled in Paris, and soon the whole metropolis, from the Royal family down to the last hysterical *bourgeoise*, were at his feet. The clergy got frightened and cried – "the Devil"! The licensed "leeches" felt an ever-growing deficit in their pockets; and the aristocracy and the Court found themselves on the verge of madness from mere excitement. No use repeating too well-known facts, but the memory of the reader may be refreshed with a few details he may have forgotten.

It so happened that just about that time the official Academical Science felt very proud. After centuries of mental stagnation in the realm of medicine and general ignorance, several determined steps in the direction of real knowledge had finally been made. Natural sciences had achieved a decided success, and chemistry and physics were on a fair way to progress. As the *Savants* of a century ago had not yet grown to that height of sublime modesty which characterizes so pre-eminently their modern successors – they felt very much puffed up with their greatness. The moment for praiseworthy humility, followed by a confession of the relative insignificance of the knowledge of the period – and even of modern knowledge for the matter of that – compared to that which the ancients knew, had not yet arrived. Those were days of naive boasting of the peacocks of science displaying in a body their tails, and demanding universal recognition and admiration. The Sir Oracles were not as numerous as they are now, yet their number was considerable. And indeed, had not the Dulcamaras of public fairs been just visited with ostracism? Had not the *leeches* well nigh disappeared to make room for diploma-ed physicians with royal licenses to kill and bury a *piacere ad libitum?* Hence, the nodding "Immortal" in his academical chair was regarded as the sole competent authority in the decision of questions he had never studied, and for rendering verdicts about that which he had never heard of. It was the REIGN OF REASON, and of Science – in its teens; the beginning of the great deadly struggle between Theology and Facts, Spirituality and Materialism. In the educated classes of Society too much faith had been succeeded by no faith at all The cycle of Science-worship had just set in, with its pilgrimages to the Academy, the Olympus where the "Forty Immortals" are enshrined, and its raids upon every one who refused to manifest a noisy admiration, a kind of juvenile calf's enthusiasm, at the door of the Fane of Science. When Mesmer arrived, Paris divided its allegiance between the Church, which attributed all kinds of phenomena except its own *divine miracles* to the Devil, and the Academy, which believed in neither God nor Devil, but only in its own infallible wisdom.

But there were minds which would not be satisfied with either of these beliefs. Therefore, after Mesmer had forced all Paris to crowd to his halls, waiting hours to obtain a place in the chair round the miraculous *baquet,* some people thought that it was time

39

real truth should be found out. They had laid their legitimate desires at the royal feet, and the King forthwith commanded his learned Academy to look into the matter. Then it was, that awakening from their chronic nap, the "Immortals" appointed a committee of investigation, among which was Benjamin Franklin, and chose some of the oldest, wisest and baldest among their "Infants" to watch over the Committee. This was in 1784. Every one knows what was the report of the latter and the final decision of the Academy. The whole transaction looks now like a general rehearsal of the play, one of the acts of which was performed by the "Dialectical Society" of London and some of England's greatest Scientists, some eighty years later.

Indeed, notwithstanding a counter report by Dr. Jussieu, an Academician of the highest rank, and the Court physician D'Eslon, who, as eye-witnesses to the most striking phenomena, demanded that a careful investigation should be made by the Medical Faculty of the therapeutic effects of the magnetic fluid – their demand fell through. The Academy disbelieved her most eminent Scientists. Even Sir B. Franklin, so much at home with cosmic electricity, would not recognize its fountain head and primordial source, and along with Bailly, Lavoisier, Magendie, and others, proclaimed Mesmerism a delusion. Nor had the second investigation which followed the first – namely in 1825 – any better results. The report was once more squashed *(vide* "Isis Unveiled," vol. i, pp. 171-176).

Even now when experiment has amply demonstrated that "Mesmerism" or animal magnetism, now known as hypnotism (*a sorry effect, forsooth, of the "Breath of Cybele"*) is *a fact,* we yet get the majority of scientists denying its actual existence. Small fry as it is in the majestic array of experimental psycho-magnetic phenomena, even hypnotism seems too incredible, *too mysterious,* for our Darwinists and Haeckelians. One needs too much moral courage, you see, to face the suspicion of one's colleagues, the doubt of the public, and the giggling of fools. "Mystery and charlatanism go hand in hand," they say; and "self-respect and the dignity of the profession," as Magendie remarks in his *Physiologie Humaine,* "demand that the well informed physician should remember how readily mystery glides into charlatanism." Pity the "well informed physician" should fail to remember that physiology among the rest is full of mystery – profound, inexplicable mystery from A to Z – and ask whether, starting from the above "truism," he should not throw overboard Biology and Physiology as the greatest pieces of charlatanry in modern Science. Nevertheless, a few in the well-meaning minority of our physicians have taken up seriously the investigation of hypnotism. But even they, having been reluctantly compelled to confess the reality of its phenomena, still persist in seeing in such manifestations no higher a factor at work than the purely material and physical forces, and deny these their legitimate name of animal magnetism. But as the Rev. Mr. Haweis (*of whom more presently*) just said in the *Daily Graphic* . . . "The Charcot phenomena are, for all that, in many ways identical with the mesmeric phenomena, and hypnotism must properly be considered rather as a branch of mesmerism than as something distinct from it. Anyhow, Mesmer's facts, now generally accepted, were at first stoutly denied." And they are still so denied.

But while they deny Mesmerism, they rush into Hypnotism, despite the now scientifically recognized dangers of this science, in which medical practitioners in France are far ahead of the English. And what the former say is, that between the two states of mesmerism (*or magnetism as they call it, across the water*) and hypnotism "there is an abyss." That one is beneficent, the other maleficent, as it evidently must be; since, according to both Occultism and modern Psychology, *hypnotism is produced by the withdrawal of the nervous fluid from the capillary nerves,* which being, so to say, the sentries that keep the doors of our senses opened, getting *anaesthetized* under hypnotic conditions, allow these to get closed. A. H. Simonin reveals many a wholesome truth in his excellent work, "Solution du probleme de la suggestion hypnotique." Thus he shows that while "in Magnetism (*mesmerism*) there occurs in the *subject* a great development of moral faculties"; that his thoughts and feelings "become loftier, and the senses acquire an abnormal acuteness"; in hypnotism, on the contrary, "the subject becomes *a simple mirror.*" It is Suggestion which is the true motor of every action in the hypnotic: and if, occasionally, "seemingly marvelous actions are produced, these are due to the hypnotizer, not to the subject." Again . . . "In hypnotism instinct, *i.e.,* the *animal,* reaches its greatest development; so much so, indeed, that the aphorism 'extremes meet' can never receive a better application than to magnetism and hypnotism." How true these words, also, as to the difference between the mesmerized and the hypnotized subjects. "In one, his ideal nature, his moral self – the reflection of his divine nature – are carried to their extreme limits, and the subject becomes almost a celestial being *(un ange)*. In the other, it is his *instincts* which develop in a most surprising fashion. The hypnotic lowers himself to the level of the animal. From a physiological standpoint, magnetism (*mesmerism*) is comforting and curative, and hypnotism, which is but the result of an unbalanced state, is – most dangerous."

Thus the adverse Report drawn by Bailly at the end of last century has had dire effects in the present, but it had its *Karma* also. Intended to kill the "Mesmeric" *craze,* it reacted as a death-blow to the public confidence in scientific decrees. In our day the *Non-Possumus* of the Royal Colleges and Academies is quoted on the Stock Exchange of the world's opinion at a price almost as low as the *Non-Possumus* of the Vatican. The days of authority whether human or divine, are fast gliding away; and we see already gleaming on future horizons but one tribunal, supreme and final, before which mankind will bow – the Tribunal of Fact and Truth.

Aye, to this tribunal without appeal even liberal clergymen and famous preachers make obeisance in our day. The parts have now changed hands, and in many instances it is the successors of those who fought tooth and nail for the reality of the Devil and his direct interference with psychic phenomena, for long centuries, who come out publicly to upbraid science. A remarkable instance of this is found in an excellent letter (*just mentioned*) by the Rev. Mr. Haweis to the *Graphic*. The learned preacher seems to share our indignation at the unfairness of the modern scientists, at their suppression of truth, and ingratitude to their ancient teachers. His letter is so interesting that its best points must be immortalized in our magazine. Here are some fragments of it. Thus he asks: –

Why can't our scientific men say: "We have blundered about Mesmerism; it's practically true"? Not because they are men of science, but simply because they are human. No doubt it is humiliating when you have dogmatized in the name of science to say, "I was wrong." But is it not more humiliating to be found out; and is it not most humiliating, after shuffling and wriggling hopelessly in the inexorable meshes of serried facts, to collapse suddenly, and call the hated net a "suitable enclosure," in which forsooth, you don't mind being caught? Now this, as it seems to me, is precisely what Messrs. Charcot and the French hypnotists and their medical admirers in England are doing. Ever since Mesmer's death at the age of eighty, in 1815, the French and English "Faculty," with some honorable exceptions, have ridiculed and denied the facts as well as the theories of Mesmer, but now, in 1890, a host of scientists suddenly agree, while wiping out as best they may the name of Mesmer, to rob him of all his phenomena, which they quietly appropriate under the name of "hypnotism," "suggestion," "Therapeutic Magnetism," "psychopathic Massage," and all the rest of it. Well, "What's in a name?"

I care more for things than names, but I reverence the pioneers of thought who have been cast out, trodden under foot, and crucified by the orthodox of all ages, and I think the least scientists can do for men like Mesmer, Du Potet, Puysegur, or Mayo and Elliotson, now they are gone, is to "build their sepulchres."

But Mr. Haweis might have added instead, the amateur Hypnotists of Science dig with their own hands the graves of many a man and woman's intellect; they enslave and paralyze freewill in their "subjects," turn immortal men into soulless, irresponsible automata, and vivisect *their souls* with as much unconcern as they vivisect the bodies of rabbits and dogs. In short, they are fast blooming into "sorcerers," and are turning science into a vast field of black magic. The rev. writer, however, lets the culprits off easily; and, remarking that he accepts "the distinction" (between Mesmerism and Hypnotism) "without pledging himself to any theory," he adds: –

I am mainly concerned with the facts, and what I want to know is why these cures and abnormal states are trumpeted about as modern discoveries, while the "faculty" still deride or ignore their great predecessors without having themselves a theory which they can agree upon or a single fact which can be called new. The truth is we are just blundering back with toil to work over again the old disused mines of the ancients; the rediscovery of these occult sciences is exactly matched by the slow recovery of sculpture and painting in modern Europe. Here is the history of occult science in a nutshell. (1) Once known. (2) Lost. (3) Rediscovered. (4) Denied. (5) Reaffirmed, and by slow degrees, under new names, victorious. The evidence for all this is exhaustive and abundant. Here it may suffice to notice that Diodorus Siculus mentions how the Egyptian priests, ages before Christ, attributed clairvoyance induced for therapeutic purposes to Isis. Strabo ascribes the same to Serapis, while Galen mentions a temple near Memphis famous for these Hypnotic cures. Pythagoras, who won the confidence of the Egyptian priests, is full of it. Aristophanes in "Plutus" describes in some detail a Mesmeric cure – "and first he began to handle the head." Caelius Aurelianus describes manipulations (1569) for disease "conducting the hands from the superior to the inferior parts"; and there was an old Latin proverb – *Ubi dolor ibi digitus,* "Where pain there finger." But time would fail me to tell of Paracelsus (1462) and his "deep secret of Magnetism"; of Van Helmont (1644) and his "faith in the power of the hand in disease." Much in the writings of both these men was only made clear to the moderns by *the experiments of Mesmer,* and in view of modern Hypnotists it is clearly with him and his disciples that we have chiefly to do. He claimed, no doubt, to transmit an animal magnetic fluid, which I believe the Hypnotists deny.

They do, they do. But so did the scientists with regard to more than one truth. To deny "an animal magnetic fluid" is surely no more absurd than to deny the circulation of the blood, as they have so energetically done.

A few additional details about Mesmerism given by Mr. Haweis may prove interesting. Thus he reminds us of the answer written by the much wronged Mesmer to the Academicians after their unfavorable Report, and refers to it as "prophetic words."

"You say that Mesmer will never hold up his head again. If such is the destiny of the man it is not the destiny of the truth, which is in its nature imperishable, and will shine forth sooner or later in the same or some other country with more brilliancy than ever, and its triumph will annihilate its miserable detractors." Mesmer left Paris in disgust, and retired to Switzerland to die; but the illustrious Dr. Jussieu became a convert. Lavater carried Mesmer's system to Germany, while Puysegur and Deleuze spread it throughout provincial France, forming innumerable "harmonic societies" devoted to the study of therapeutic magnetism and its allied phenomena of thought-transference, hypnotism, and clairvoyance.

Some twenty years ago I became acquainted with perhaps the most illustrious disciple of Mesmer, the aged Baron du Potet. Round this man's therapeutic and mesmeric exploits raged, between 1830 and 1846, a bitter controversy throughout France. A murderer had been tracked, convicted, and executed solely on evidence supplied by one of Du Potet's clairvoyants. The Juge de Paix admitted thus much in open court. This was too much for even skeptical Paris, and the Academy determined to sit again and, if possible, crush out the superstition. They sat, but, strange to say, this time they were converted. Itard, Fouquier, Guersent, Bourdois de la Motte, the cream of the French faculty, pronounced the phenomena of mesmerism to be genuine — cures, trances, clairvoyance, thought-transference, even reading from closed books; and from that time an elaborate nomenclature was invented, blotting out as far as possible the detested names of the indefatigable men who had compelled the scientific assent, while enrolling the main facts vouched for by Mesmer, Du Potet, and Puysegur among the undoubted phenomena to be accepted, on whatever theory, by medical science. . . .

Then comes the turn of this foggy island and its befogged scientists. "Meanwhile," goes on the writer,

England was more stubborn. In 1846 the celebrated Dr. Elliot son, a popular practitioner, with a vast *clientele,* pronounced the famous Harveian oration, in which he confessed his belief in Mesmerism. He was denounced by the doctors with such thorough results that he lost his practice, and died well-nigh ruined, if not heart-broken. The Mesmeric Hospital in Marylebone Road has been established by him. Operations were successfully performed under Mesmerism, and all the phenomena which have lately occurred at Leeds and elsewhere to the satisfaction of the doctors were produced in Marylebone fifty-six years ago. Thirty-five years ago Professor Lister did the same – but the introduction of chloroform being more speedy and certain as an anesthetic, killed for a time the mesmeric treatment. The public interest in Mesmerism died down, and the Mesmeric Hospital in the Marylebone Road, which had been under a cloud since the suppression of Elliotson, was at last closed. Lately we know what has been the fate of Mesmer and Mesmerism. Mesmer is spoken of in the same breath with Count Cagliostro, and Mesmerism itself is seldom mentioned at all; but, then, we hear plenty of electro-biology, therapeutic magnetism and hypnotism – just so. Oh, shades of Mesmer, Puysegur, Du Potet, Elliotson – *sic vos non vobis*. Still, I say *Palmam qui meruit ferat*. When I knew Baron du Potet he was on the brink of the grave, and nearly eighty years old. He was an ardent admirer of Mesmer; he had devoted his whole life to therapeutic magnetism, and he was absolutely dogmatic on the point that a real magnetic aura passed from the Mesmerist to the patient. "I will show you this," he said one day, as we both stood by the bedside of a patient in so deep a trance that we ran needles into her hands and arms without exciting the least sign or movement. The old Baron continued: "I will, at the distance of a foot or two, determine slight convulsions in any part of her body by simply moving my hand above the part, without any contact." He began at the shoulder, which soon set up a twitching. Quiet being restored, he tried the elbow, then the wrist, then the knee, the convulsions increasing in intensity according to the time employed. "Are you quite satisfied?" I said, "Quite satisfied"; and, continued he, "any patient that I have tested I will undertake to operate upon through a brick wall at a time and place where the patient shall be ignorant of my presence or my purpose. This," added Du Potet, "was one of the experiences which most puzzled the Academicians at Paris. I repeated the experiment again and again under every test and condition, with almost invariable success, until the most skeptical was forced to give in."

We have accused science of gliding full sail down to the Maelstrom of Black Magic, by practicing that which ancient Psychology – the most important branch of the Occult Sciences – has always declared as Sorcery in its application to the *inner* man. We are prepared to maintain what we say. We mean to prove it one of these days, in some future articles, basing ourselves on facts published and the actions produced by the Hypnotism of Vivisectionists themselves. That they are unconscious sorcerers does not make away with the fact that they do practice the Black Art *bel et bien*. In short the situation is this. The minority of the learned physicians and other scientists experiment in "hypnotism" because they have come to see something in it; while the majority of the members of the R.C.P.'s still deny the actuality of animal magnetism in its mesmeric form, even under its modern mask – hypnotism. The former – entirely ignorant of the fundamental laws of animal magnetism – experiment at haphazard, almost blindly. To remain consistent with their declarations *(a)* that hypnotism is *not* mesmerism, and *(b)* that a magnetic aura or fluid passing from the mesmerizer (*or hypnotizer*) is pure fallacy – they have no right, of course, to apply the laws of the older to the younger science. Hence they interfere with, and awaken to action the most dangerous forces of nature, without being aware of it. Instead of healing diseases – the only use to which animal magnetism under its new name can be *legitimately* applied – they often inoculate the *subjects with* their own physical as well as mental ills and vices. For this, and the ignorance of their colleagues of the minority, the disbelieving majority of the Sadducees are greatly responsible. For, by opposing them, they impede free action, and take advantage of the Hippocratic oath, to make them powerless to admit and do much that the believers might and would otherwise do. But as Dr. A. Teste truly says in his work – "*There are certain unfortunate truths which compromise those who believe in them, and those especially who are so candid as to avow them publicly.*" Thus the reason of hypnotism not being studied on its proper lines is self-evident.

Years ago it was remarked: "It is the duty of the Academy and medical authorities to study Mesmerism *(i.e.,* the occult sciences in its spirit) and to subject it to trials; finally, to *take away the use and practice of it from persons quite strangers to the art, who abuse this means, and make it an object of lucre and speculation."* He who uttered this great truth was "the voice speaking in the desert." But those having some experience in occult psychology would go further. They would say it is incumbent on every scientific body – nay, on *every* government – to put an end to public exhibitions of this sort. By trying the *magic* effect of the human will on weaker wills, by deriding the existence of *occult* forces in Nature – forces whose name is legion – and yet calling out these, under the pretext that they are *no* independent forces at all, not even psychic in their nature, but "connected with known *physical* laws" (Binet and Féré), men in authority are virtually responsible for all the dire effects that are and will be following their dangerous public experiments. Verily Karma – the terrible but just Retributive Law – will visit all those who develop the most awful results in the future, generated at those public exhibitions for the amusement of the profane. Let them only think of dangers bred, of new forms of diseases, mental and physical, begotten by such insane handling of psychic will! This is as bad on the moral plane as the artificial introduction of animal matter into the human blood, by the infamous Brown Sequard method, is on the physical. They laugh at the occult sciences and deride Mesmerism? Yet this century will not have passed away before they have undeniable proofs that the idea of a crime suggested for experiment's sake is not removed by a reversed current of the will as easily as it is inspired. They may learn that if the outward expression of the idea of a misdeed "suggested" may fade out at the will of the operator, the *active living germ* artificially implanted does not disappear with it; that once dropped into the seat of the human – or, rather, the animal – passions, it may lie dormant there for years sometimes, to become suddenly awakened by some unforeseen circumstance into realization. Crying children frightened into silence by the *suggestion* of a monster, a devil standing in the corner, by a foolish nurse, have been known to become insane twenty or thirty years later on the same subject. There are mysterious, secret drawers, dark nooks and hiding-places in the labyrinth of our memory, still unknown to physiologists, and which open only once, rarely twice, in man's lifetime, and that only under very abnormal and peculiar conditions. But when they do, it is always some heroic deed committed by a person the least calculated for it, or – a terrible crime perpetrated, the reason for which remains for ever a mystery. . . .

Thus experiments in "suggestion" by persons ignorant of the occult laws, are the most dangerous of pastimes. The action and reaction of ideas on the *inner lower* "Ego," has never been studied so far, because that Ego itself is *terra incognita* (even when not denied) to the men of science. Moreover, such performances before a promiscuous public are a danger in themselves. Men of undeniable scientific education who experiment on Hypnotism in public, lend thereby the sanction of their names to such performances. And then every unworthy speculator acute enough to understand the process may, by developing by practice and perseverance the same force in himself, apply it to his own selfish, often criminal, ends. *Result on Karmic lines:* every Hypnotist, every man of Science, however well-meaning and honorable, once he has allowed himself to become the unconscious instructor of one who learns but to abuse the sacred science, becomes, of course, morally the confederate of every crime committed by this means.

Such is the consequence of public "Hypnotic" experiments which thus lead to, and virtually are, BLACK MAGIC.

AFRICAN MAGIC

Before we enter into the subject of the occult art as practised on the West Coast of Africa, it will be well to clear the ground by first considering for a moment what we mean by the much abused term "Magic."

There are many definitions of this word; and, in bygone ages, it was simply used to designate anything and everything which was "not understood of the vulgar". It will be sufficient for our purpose to define it as the knowledge of certain natural laws which are not merely unknown but absolutely unsuspected by the scientists of Europe and America.

It is a recognised fact that no law of Nature can be—even for a single moment—abrogated. When, therefore, this appears to be the case—when, for instance, such a universally known law as that of the attraction of gravitation seems to be annihilated, we must recognise the fact that there may be other laws at present unknown to Western science which have the power of overriding and suspending for the time being the action of the known law.

The knowledge of these hidden laws is what we understand by the term occult science or magic.

And there is no other magic than this, and never has been, at any period of the world's history. All the so-called "miracles" of ancient times can be and are reproduced at the present day by magists when occasion requires. An act of magic is a pure scientific feat, and must not be confounded with legerdemain or trickery or any kind.

There are several schools of magism, all proceeding and operating on entirely different lines. The principal of these, and on whose philosophy all others are founded, are the Hindu, the Thibetan, the Egyptian (including the Arab) and the Obeeyan or Voodoo. The last named is entirely and fundamentally opposed to the other three: it having its root and foundation in necromancy or "black magic", while the others all operate either by means of what is known to experts as "white magic", or in other cases by "psychologizing" the spectator. And, a whole crowd of spectators can be psychologized and made at the will of the operator to see and feel whatever things he chooses, all the time being in full possession of their ordinary faculties. Thus, perhaps a couple of travelling fakirs give their performance in your own compound or in the garden of your bungalow. They erect a small tent and tell you to choose any animal which you wish to see emerge therefrom. Many different animals are named in rotation by the bystanders, and in every case the desired quadruped, be he tiger or terrier dog, comes out of the opening in the canvas and slowly marches off until he disappears round some adjacent corner. Well, this is done simply by "psychologizing", as are all the other great Indian feats, such as the "basket trick", "the mango tree", throwing a rope in the air and climbing up it, pulling it up and disappearing in space, and the thousand and one other similar performances which are "familiar as household words" to almost every Anglo-Indian.

The difference between these schools and that of the Voodoo or Obeeyah is very great, because in them there is a deception or want of reality in the performance. The spectator does not really see what he fancies he sees: his mind is simply impressed by the operator and the effect is produced. But in African magic, on the contrary, there is no will impression: the observer does really and actually see what is taking place. The force employed by the African necromancers is not psychological action, but demonosophy.

White magists have frequently dominated and employed inferior spirits to do their bidding, as well as invoked the aid of powerful and beneficent ones to carry out their purposes.

But this is an entirely different thing: The spirits which are naturally maleficent become the slaves of the magist, and he controls them and compels them to carry out his beneficent plans. The necromancer, or votary of black magic, is, on the contrary, the slave of the evil spirit to whom he has given himself up.

While the philosophy of the magist demands a life of the greatest purity and the practice of every virtue, while he must utterly subdue and have in perfect control all his desires and appetites, mental and physical, and must became simply an embodied intellect, absolutely purged from all human weakness and pusillanimity, the necromancer must outrage and degrade human nature in every way conceivable. The very least of the crimes necessary for him (or her) to commit to attain the power sought is actual murder, by which the human victim essential to the sacrifice is provided. The human mind can scarcely realise or even imagine one tithe of the horrors and atrocities actually performed by the Obeeyah women.

Yet, though the price is awful, horrible, unutterable, the power is real. There is no possibility of mistake about that. Every petty king on the West Coast has his "rain-maker". It is the fashion among travellers, and the business of the missionaries, to ridicule and deny the powers of these people. But they do possess and do actually use the power of causing storms of rain, wind, and lightning. When one considers that however ignorant and brutal a savage may be, yet that he has an immense amount of natural cunning, and his very ignorance makes him believe nothing that cannot be proved to him, no "rain-maker" could live for one year unless he gave repeated instances of his powers when required by the king. Failure would simply mean death. And the hypothesis that they only work their conjurations when the weather is on the point of change is only an invention of the missionaries. The native chiefs are, like all savages, able to detect an approaching change of weather many hours before it takes place. And is it at all likely that they would send for the rain-maker and give him sufficient cattle to last him for twelve months, besides wives and other luxuries, if there were the slightest appearance of approaching rain?

I remember well my first experience of these wizards. For weeks and weeks there had been no rain, although it was the rainy season. The mealies were all dying for want of water; the cattle being slaughtered in all directions; women and children had died by scores, and the fighting men were beginning to do the same, being themselves scarcely more than skeletons. Day after day, the sun glared down on the parched earth, without one intervening cloud, like a globe of glowing copper, and all Nature languished in that awful furnace. Suddenly the king ordered the great war drum to be beaten, and the warriors all gathered hurriedly. He announced the arrival of two celebrated rain-makers, who would forthwith proceed to relieve the prevailing distress. The elder of the two was a stunted, bow-legged little man, with wool which would have been white had it not been messed up with grease, filth and feathers. The second was rather a fine specimen of the Soosoo race, but with a very sinister expression. A large ring being formed by the squatting negroes, who came—for some unknown reason—all armed to the teeth, the king being in the centre, and the rain-makers in front of him, they commenced their incantations. The zenith and the horizon were eagerly examined from time to time, but not a vestige of a cloud appeared. Presently the elder man rolled on the ground in convulsions, apparently epileptic, and his comrade started to his feet pointing with both hands to the copper-colored sky. All eyes followed his gesture, and looked at the spot to which his hands pointed, but nothing was visible. Motionless as a stone statue he stood with gaze rivetted on the sky. In about the space of a minute a darker shade was observable in the copper tint, in another minute it grew darker and darker, and, in a few more seconds developed into a black cloud, which soon overspread the heavens. In a moment, a vivid flash was seen, and the deluge that fell from that cloud, which had now spread completely overhead, was something to be remembered. For two days and nights that torrent poured down, and seemed as if it would wash everything out of the ground.

After the king had dismissed the rain-makers, and they had deposited the cattle and presents under guard, I entered the hut in which they were lodged, and spent the night with them, discussing the magical art. The hut was about fourteen feet in diameter, strongly built of posts driven firmly into the ground, and having a strong thatched conical roof. I eventually persuaded them to give me one or two examples of their skill. They began singing, or rather crooning, a long invocation, after a few minutes of which the younger man appeared to rise in the air about three feet from the ground and remain there unsuspended, and floating about. There was a brilliant light in the hut from a large fire in the centre, so that the smallest detail could be distinctly observed. I got up and went to feel the man in the air, and there was no doubt about his levitation. He then floated close to the wall and passed through it to the outside. I made a dash for the doorway, which was on the opposite side of the hut, and looked round for him. I saw a luminous figure which appeared like a man rubbed with phosphorised oil; but I was glad to rapidly take shelter from the torrents of rain. When I re-entered the hut, there was only the old man present. I examined the logs carefully, but there was no aperture whatever. The old man continued his chant, and in another moment his comrade re-appeared floating in the air. He sat down on the ground, and I saw his black skin glistening with rain, and the few rags he wore were as wet as if he had been dipped in a river.

The next feat was performed by the old man, and consisted in several instantaneous disappearances and reappearances. The curious point about this was that the old man also was dripping wet.

Following this was a very interesting exhibition. By the old man's directions we arranged ourselves round the fire at the three points of an imaginary triangle. The men waved their hands over the fire in rhythm with their chant when dozens of tic-polongas, the most deadly serpent in Africa, slowly crawled out from the burning embers, and interlacing themselves together whirled in a mad dance on their tails round the fire, making all the while a continuous hissing. At the word of command they all sprang into the fire and disappeared. The young man then came round to me, and, kneeling down, opened his mouth, out of which the head of a tic-polonga was quickly protruded. He snatched it out, pulling a serpent nearly three feet long out of his throat, and threw it also into the fire. In rapid succession he drew seven serpents from his throat, and consigned them all to the same fiery end.

But I wanted to know what they could do in the way of evocation of spirits. The incantation this time lasted nearly twenty minutes, when, rising slowly from the fire, appeared a human figure, a man of great age, a white man too, but absolutely nude. I put several questions to him, but obtained no reply. I arose and walked round the fire, and particularly noticed a livid scar on his back. I could get no satisfactory explanation of who he was, but they seemed rather afraid of him, and had evidently—from the remarks they interchanged—expected to see a black man.

After the appearance of this white man, I could not persuade them that night to attempt anything more, although the next night I had no difficulty with them. A most impressive feat, which they on a subsequent occasion performed, was the old custom of the priests of Taal. Commencing a lugubrious chant they slowly began circling around the fire (which said fire always is an essential part of the proceedings), keeping a certain amount of rhythm in both their movements and cadences. Presently, the movement grew faster and faster till they whirled round like dancing dervishes. There were two distinct movements; all the time during which they were gyrating round the circle, they were rapidly spinning on their own axes. With the rapidity of their evolutions their voices were raised higher and higher until the din was terrific. Then, by a simultaneous movement, each began slashing his naked body on arms, chest, and thighs, until they were streaming with blood and covered with deep gashes. Then the old man stopped his erratic course, and sitting down on the ground narrowly watched the younger one with apparent solicitude. The young man continued his frantic exertions until exhausted Nature could bear no more, and he fell panting and helpless on the ground. The old man took both the knives and anointed the blades with some evil smelling grease from a calabash, and then stroked the young man's body all over with the blade which had done the injuries, and finished the operation by rubbing him vigorously with the palms of the hands smeared with the unguent.

In a few minutes time the young man arose, and there was not the slightest trace of wound or scar in his ebony skin. He then performed the same good offices on the old man with the same effect. Within ten minutes afterwards they were both laid on their mats in a sweet and quiet sleep. In this performance there were many invocations, gestures, the circular fire, and other things which satisfied me that some portion, at all events, of the magical processes of West Africa had been handed down from the days when Baal was an actual God, and mighty in the land.

www.ingramcontent.com/pod-product-compliance
Lightning Source LLC
LaVergne TN
LVHW041459070426
835507LV00009B/684